O TASTE AND SEE

By the same author

The Double Image

Here and Now

Overland to the Islands

With Eyes at the Back of Our Heads

The Jacob's Ladder

new poems by

Denise Levertov

O Taste and See

A New Directions Book

Some of the material in this book first appeared in the following
magazines, to which acknowledgement is gratefully made:
*Beloit Poetry Journal, Harper's Bazaar, Massachusetts Review,
Minnesota Review, The New Review, Nomad, Origin, Paris
Review, Poetry* (Chicago), *Rivoli Review, Wagner College
Literary Magazine, Burning Deck, The New Statesman, Emer-
son Review, Genesis West, The Nation, Sturbridge, Wild Dog,
Granta* and *Hudson Review.*

"The Breathing" was first published in *Poetry in Crystal* by
Steuben Glass.

Title page photograph by Roloff Beny

Published simultaneously in Canada by McClelland & Stewart, Ltd.

Manufactured in the United States of America.

New Directions Books are published by James Laughlin at
Norfolk, Connecticut. New York office: 333 Sixth Avenue
(14).

Most of these poems were written during the year I was a Guggenheim Fellow. I would like to thank the John Simon Guggenheim Foundation and its administrators for giving me this opportunity.

DENISE LEVERTOV

Contents

O TASTE AND SEE

The moon is a sow
and grunts in my throat
Her great shining shines through me
so the mud of my hollow gleams
and breaks in silver bubbles

She is a sow
and I a pig and a poet

When she opens her white
lips to devour me I bite back
and laughter rocks the moon

In the black of desire
we rock and grunt, grunt and
shine

Elves are no smaller
than men, and walk
as men do, in this world,
but with more grace than most,
and are not immortal.

Their beauty sets them aside
from other men and from women
unless a woman has that cold fire in her
called poet: with that

she may see them and by its light
they know her and are not afraid
and silver tongues of love
flicker between them.

The ache of marriage:

thigh and tongue, beloved,
are heavy with it,
it throbs in the teeth

We look for communion
and are turned away, beloved,
each and each

It is leviathan and we
in its belly
looking for joy, some joy
not to be known outside it

two by two in the ark of
the ache of it.

Your beauty, which I lost sight of once
for a long time, is long,
not symmetrical, and wears
the earth colors that make me see it.

A long beauty, what is that?
A song
that can be sung over and over,
long notes or long bones.

Love is a landscape the long mountains
define but don't
shut off from the
unseeable distance.

In fall, in fall,
your trees stretch
their long arms in sleeves
of earth-red and

sky-yellow. I take
long walks among them. The grapes
that need frost to ripen them

are amber and grow deep in the
hedge, half-concealed,
the way your beauty grows in long tendrils
half in darkness.

Cross-country, out of sea fog
comes a letter in dream: a Bard
claims from me 'on whose land they grow,'
seeds of the forget-me-not.

'I ask you
to gather them for me,' says
the Spirit of Poetry.
                    The varied blue
in small compass. In multitude
a cloud of blue, a river
beside the brown river.

Not flowers but
their seeds, I am to send him.
And he bids me
remember my nature, speaking of it
as of a power.
And gather
the flowers, and the flowers
of 'labor' (pink in the dream,
a bright centaury with more petals.
Or the form changes to a sea-pink.)

Ripple of blue in which are
distinct blues. Bold
centaur-seahorse-salt-carnation
flower of work and transition.
Out of sea fog, from a hermitage,
at break of day.

Shall I find them, then—
here on my own land, recalled
to my nature?
                    O, great Spirit!

7

An absolute
patience.
Trees stand
up to their knees in
fog. The fog
slowly flows
uphill.
        White
cobwebs, the grass
leaning where deer
have looked for apples.
The woods
from brook to where
the top of the hill looks
over the fog, send up
not one bird.
So absolute, it is
no other than
happiness itself, a breathing
too quiet to hear.

This is the year the old ones,
the old great ones
leave us alone on the road.

The road leads to the sea.
We have the words in our pockets,
obscure directions. The old ones

have taken away the light of their presence,
we see it moving away over a hill
off to one side.

They are not dying,
they are withdrawn
into a painful privacy

learning to live without words.
E.P. "It looks like dying"—Williams: "I can't
describe to you what has been

happening to me"—
H.D. "unable to speak."
The darkness

twists itself in the wind, the stars
are small, the horizon
ringed with confused urban light-haze.

They have told us
the road leads to the sea,
and given

the language into our hands.
We hear
our footsteps each time a truck

has dazzled past us and gone
leaving us new silence.
One can't reach

the sea on this endless
road to the sea unless
one turns aside at the end, it seems,

follows
the owl that silently glides above it
aslant, back and forth,

and away into deep woods.

But for us the road
unfurls itself, we count the
words in our pockets, we wonder

how it will be without them, we don't
stop walking, we know
there is far to go, sometimes

we think the night wind carries
a smell of the sea. . .

Paradise, an
endless movie. You
walk in, sit down in the dark, it
draws you into itself.

Slowly
an old man crosses
the field of vision, his passions
gathering to the brim of his soul.
And grasses
bow and straighten,

the pulse of wind irregular,
gleam of twilight.

Anything, the attention
never wavers. A woman, say,
who is sleeping or laughing or making
coffee.
A marriage.

Stir of time, the sequence
returning upon itself, branching
a new way. To suffer, pains, hope.
The attention
lives in it as a poem lives or a song
going under the skin of memory.

Or, to believe it's there
within you
though the key's missing

makes it enough? As if
golden pollen were falling

onto your hair from dark trees.

On white linen the silk
of gray shadows
threefold, over-
lapping, a
tau cross.
Glass jug and
tumblers rise from
that which they
cast.

And luminous
in each
overcast of
cylindrical shade,
image
of water, a brightness
not gold, not silver,
rippling
as if with laughter.

In today's mail a poem
quotes from Ecclesiastes:
**Whatsoever thy hand
findeth to do, do it with thy might:
for there is no work,
nor device,
nor knowledge,
nor wisdom,
in the grave, whither thou goest.**
A letter with it
discloses, in its words and between them,
a life opening, fearful, fearless,
thousand-eyed, a field
of sparks that move swiftly
in darkness, to and from
a center. He is beginning
to live.
The threat
of world's end is the old threat.
'**Prepare
for the world to come as thou shouldest
die tomorrow**' says
the Book of Delight,
and:
'**Prepare for this world as thou
shouldst live forever.**'

In the gold mouth of a flower
the black smell of spring earth.
No more skulls on our desks

but the pervasive
testing of death—as if we had need
of new ways of dying? No,

we have no need
of new ways of dying.
Death in us goes on

testing the wild
chance of living
as Adam chanced it.

Golden-mouth, the tilted smile
of the moon westering
is at the black window,

Calavera of Spring.
Do you mistake me?
I am speaking of living,

of moving from one moment into
the next, and into the
one after, breathing

death in the spring air, knowing
air also means
music to sing to.

Turtle Goddess
she of the hard shell
soft underneath
awaits enormously
in a dark grotto
the young Heroes—

Then the corridor
of booths—in each
Life enshrined in
veils of light, scenes
of bliss or
dark action.
Honey and fog, the nose
confused.

And at the corridor's end
two steps
down into Nothing—

The film is over
we're out in the street—

The film-maker's wife grieves and tells him
good-by for ever, you were wrong,
wrong to have shown the Turtle Mother.
The darkness
should not be revealed.
Farewell.

Maker of visions
he walks with me
to the gate of Home and leaves me.
I enter.

18

Mother is gone,
only Things remain.

So be it.

The pastor
of grief and dreams

guides his flock towards
the next field

with all his care.
He has heard

the bell tolling
but the sheep

are hungry and need
the grass, today and

every day. Beautiful
his patience, his long

shadow, the rippling
sound of the flock moving

along the valley.

Two girls discover
the secret of life
in a sudden line of
poetry.

I who don't know the
secret wrote
the line. They
told me

(through a third person)
they had found it
but not what it was
not even

what line it was. No doubt
by now, more than a week
later, they have forgotten
the secret,

the line, the name of
the poem. I love them
for finding what
I can't find,

and for loving me
for the line I wrote,
and for forgetting it
so that

a thousand times, till death
finds them, they may
discover it again, in other
lines

in other
happenings. And for
wanting to know it,
for

assuming there is
such a secret, yes,
for that
most of all.

The cave downstairs,
jet, obsidian, ember
of bloodstone, glisten
of mineral green.
And what
hangs out there
asleep.

If a serpent were singing,
what silence.
Sleeping, sleeping,
it is the
thunder of the serpent
drumroll of
the mounting smell of

gas.
Unable to wake, to
blurt out the unworded
warning. . .

Augh!

Transformed.
A silence
of waking at night into speech.

He says the waves in the ship's wake
are like stones rolling away.
I don't see it that way.
But I see the mountain turning,
turning away its face as the ship
takes us away.

I have heard it said,
and by a wise man,
that you are not one who comes and goes

but having chosen
you remain in your human house,
and walk

in its garden for air and the delights
of weather and seasons.

Who builds
a good fire in his hearth
shall find you at it
with shining eyes and a ready tongue.

Who shares
even water and dry bread with you
will not eat without joy

and wife or husband
who does not lock the door of the marriage
against you, finds you

not as unwelcome third in the room, but as
the light of the moon on flesh and hair.

He told me, that wise man,
that when it seemed the house was
empty of you,

the fire crackling for no one,
the bread hard to swallow in solitude,
the gardens a tedious maze,

25

you were not gone away
but hiding yourself in secret rooms.
The house is no cottage, it seems,

it has stairways, corridors, cellars,
a tower perhaps,
unknown to the host.

The host, the housekeeper, it is
who fails you. He had forgotten
to make room for you at the hearth
or set a place for you at the table
or leave the doors unlocked for you.

Noticing you are not there
(when did he last see you?)
he cries out you are faithless,

have failed him,
writes you stormy letters demanding you return
it is intolerable

to maintain this great barracks without your presence,
it is too big, it is too small, the walls
menace him, the fire smokes

and gives off no heat. But to what address
can he mail the letters?
                              And all the while

you are indwelling,
a gold ring lost in the house.
A gold ring lost in the house.
You are in the house!

Then what to do to find the room where you are?
Deep cave of obsidian glowing with red, with green,
with black light,
high room in the lost tower where you sit spinning,

crack in the floor where the gold ring
waits to be found?

                    No more rage but a calm face,
trim the fire, lay the table, find some
flowers for it: is that the way?
Be ready with quick sight to catch
a gleam between the floorboards,

there, where he had looked
a thousand times and seen nothing?
                    Light of the house,

the wise man spoke
words of comfort. You are near,
perhaps you are sleeping and don't hear.

Not even a wise man
can say, do thus and thus, that presence
will be restored.
                    Perhaps

a becoming aware a door is swinging, as if
someone had passed through the room a moment ago—perhaps
looking down, the sight
of the ring back on its finger?

While snow fell carelessly
floating indifferent in eddies of
rooftop air, circling the black
chimney cowls,

a spring night entered
my mind through the tight-closed window,
wearing

a loose Russian shirt of
light silk.
   For this, then,
that slanting
line was left, that crack, the pane
never replaced.

Old Day the gardener seemed
Death himself, or Time, scythe in hand

by the sundial and freshly-dug
grave in my book of parables.

The mignonette, the dusty miller and silvery
rocks in the garden next door

thrived in his care (the rocks
not hidden by weeds but clear-

cut between tufts
of fern and saxifrage). Now

by our peartree with pruning-hook,
now digging the Burnes's neat, weedless

rosebeds, or as he peered
at a bird in Mrs. Peach's laburnum,

his tall stooped person appeared, and gray
curls. He worked

slow and in silence, and knew perhaps
every garden around the block, gardens

we never saw, each one,
bounded by walls of old brick,

a square plot that was
world to itself.

When I was grown
and gone from home he remembered me

in the time of my growing, and sent,
year by year, salutations,

until there was no one there, in
changed times, to send them by. Old Day,

old Death, dusty
gardener, are you

alive yet, do I live on
yet, in your gray

considering eye?

In June the bush we call
alder was heavy, listless,
its leaves studded with galls,

growing wherever we didn't
want it. We cut it
savagely, hunted it from the pasture, chopped it

away from the edge of the wood.
In July, still everywhere, it appeared
wearing green berries.

Anyway it must go. It takes
the light and air and the good of the earth
from flowers and young trees.

But now in August
its berries are red. Do the birds
eat them?   Swinging

clusters of red, the hedges are full of them,
red-currant red, a graceful
ornament or a merry smile.

Quick! there's that
low brief **whirr** to tell

Rubythroat is at the
tigerlilies—

only a passionate baby
sucking breastmilk's so

intent. **Look
sharply after your thoughts** said
Emerson, a good
dreamer.

**Worlds may lie
between you
and the bird's return.** Hummingbird

stays for a fractional sharp
sweetness, and's gone, can't take

more than that.
The remaining
tigerblossoms have rolled their petals
all the way back,

the stamens protrude entire,
there are no more buds.

To come to the river
the brook
hurtles through rainy
woods, over-
topping rocks that
before the rain were
islands.

Its clearness
is gone, and
the song.
It is a rich brown, a load
of churned earth
goes with it.

The sound now
is a direct, intense
sound of
direction.

A deep wooden note
when the wind blows,
the west wind.
The rock maple is it,
close to the house?
Or a beam, voice
of the house itself?
A groan, but not
gloomy, rather
an escaped note of
almost unbearable
satisfaction, a great
bough or beam
unaware it had
spoken.

i

The All-Day Bird, the artist,
whitethroated sparrow,
striving
in hope and
good faith to make his notes
ever more precise, closer
to what he knows.

ii

There is the proposition
and the development.
The way
one grows from the other.
The All-Day Bird
ponders.

iii

May the first note
be round enough
and those that follow
fine, fine as
sweetgrass,
         prays
the All-Day Bird.

iv

Fine
as the tail of a lizard,
as a leaf of
chives—
the *shadow of a difference*
falling between
note and note,
a *hair's breadth*
defining them.

v

The dew is on the vineleaves.
My tree
is lit with the
break of day.

vi

Sun
light.
    Light
light light light.

A man growing old is going
down the dark stairs.
He has been speaking of the Soul
tattooed with the Law.
Of dreams
burnt in the bone.

He looks up
to the friends who lean
out of light and wine
over the well of stairs.
They ask his pardon
for the dark they can't help.

Starladen Babylon
buzzes in his blood, an ancient
pulse. The rivers
run out of Eden.
Before Adam
Adam blazes.

'It's alright,' answers
the man going down,
'it's alright—there are many
avenues, many corridors of the soul
that are dark also.
Shalom.'

The eastern sky at sunset taking
the glow of the west:
> the west a clear stillness.

The east flinging
nets of cloud
to hold the rose light a moment longer:
> the western hill dark to blackness.

The ants
on their acropolis
prepare for the night.

. . . .

The vine among the rocks
heavy with grapes

the shadows of September
among the gold glint of the grass

among shining
willow leaves the small birds moving

silent in the presence of a new season.

. . . .

In the last sunlight
human figures dark on the hill
outlined—

a fur of gold
about their shoulders and heads,
a blur defining them.

. . . .

Down by the fallen fruit in the old orchard
the air grows cold. The hill
hides the sun.

A sense of the present
rises out of earth and grass,
enters the feet, ascends

into the genitals, constricting
the breast, lightening
the head—a wisdom,

a shiver, a delight
that what is passing

is here, as if
a snake went by, green in the
gray leaves.

In hollows of the land
in faults and valleys
                    the white fog
bruised
            by blue shadows
a mirage of lakes

and in the human
faults and depths
                        silences
floating
            between night and daybreak
illusion and substance.

But is illusion
so repeated, known
                        each dawn,
silence
        suspended in the
mind's shadow

always, not substance
of a sort?
            the white
bruised
            ground-mist the mirage
of a true lake.

A woman had been picking flowers in the half-wild garden
of an old farmhouse. Before going indoors to put the flowers
in water and begin making supper, she walked around to the
back of the house and up the pasture a little way to look
across the valley at the hills. The pasture sloped steeply up
to a line of trees and a stone wall half-concealed with vines
and bushes, then beyond that up again to where the woods
began.

The woman waded through the uncut grass and the
milkweeds—not yet in flower—to a corner near the stone wall.
Beyond this point—the highest point near the house from
which to look to the eastern horizon—the ground dropped
toward the curving road in a tangle of bracken, alder, young
birches. Away across the valley, the unseen meadows of the
intervale, she could see the nearest dark green hills, strong
presences; and here and there, where these dipped, or sometimes higher than their highest ridges, another rank, green
too but lightly dusted with distance. The woman was glad to
be able to see them. She felt herself nourished by the sense
of distance, by the stillness and mass of the hills. They were
called mountains, locally; and they were almost mountains.
They had the dignity of mountains. She couldn't quite bring
herself to call them mountains, herself, having known higher
ones—towering, unforested, sharp-peaked and snowy. But
these old hills, rounded, softened by their woods, gave her
joy in any case. A few white clouds followed each other
across the sky, and their shadows moved darkly over the
hills revealing contours the full sun did not show. The after-
noon hummed with insects. The stems of the irises she had
picked near the driveway felt cool in her hand. Not far away
she could hear the voices of her son and her husband. They
were cutting brush in the upper part of the pasture.

A view of the hills and a feeling of openness around the
house were as important to her husband as to herself. This

was their first whole summer here—they had bought the old farm, its fields mostly gone back to woodland, two years ago—and he had spent most of his free time, in these first weeks of it, cutting back the alder bushes that threatened to take over the pasture. The boy liked to help him. Each day, too, they pulled up innumerable milkweeds and dug out dock and burdock from around the edges of the dooryard.

It was still hot in the fields though the shadows were lengthening. Soon they would be coming in, sweaty and hungry. She turned to go, sighing deeply with pleasure. But her last look at the horizon as she turned revealed a flaw she had not realized before: in a great dip of the ridge, to the northeast, some still more distant, and higher, hills—mountains—would have been visible from this lookout, had not a tall and full poplar tree blocked the view. She could glimpse the pale blue of them on either side of its rippling leaves.

At supper the man was speaking of the alders he had cut and meant to cut. The alders were not beautiful and grew with a weedlike insistence. If one did not keep after them they would smother everything. She agreed. There was a coarseness to the leaf, a formlessness about the whole plant, one could not love. The boy—who when this clearing of brush began a week or so before had opposed it, almost with tears, frightened of changing what was already good—was full of pride and enthusiasm for the work done that day. So far they had worked only with machetes and a pair of bush-cutters or with their bare hands, but soon they would get a man with a power-saw to come and fell some of the trees that were crowding each other out. And there were others they could fell with an axe—not wholesale but with judgment—to reveal the form of the land and give back some of the space years of neglect had stolen, the man added.

"I know one tree that needs cutting," the woman said, speaking suddenly as if she had been holding it back and the words had now pushed their way out of her by themselves.

"Where's that?" her husband asked, looking up from his plate, his fork poised.

"Well—it's up there beyond that corner . . . I'll show you. There are some far-away mountains one could see from there, but it gets in the way."

The meal continued, they talked of other things, the woman went back and forth between the kitchen and the dining table with dirty plates and dessert and coffee. She was smoking a cigarette and sitting idle while the boy cleared the table when her husband said to her, "Come out a moment and show me which tree you mean."

She looked up at him as if she had not heard what he said.

"Let's go out and look at that tree," he said.

Only a few days before they had gone to picnic near an abandoned hill farm that had seemed, the summer before, very beautiful in its dreaming solitude, as if at rest after a life of achievement; but they found a year's growth of the eager woods had begun to close it in, block the horizon. She had been melancholy there; the blackflies were biting, the grass around the old house had been long and rank, brambles had almost hidden the wellhead and the rhubarb patch. They had eaten quickly, feeling bad tempered, and left almost at once. It had made him very eager to preserve the feeling of lightness and calm there was about their own place.

The woman looked at him and stood up, brushing away a slight unease she felt.

"Come on out with us," the man said to the boy, who was scraping the plates over a box of garbage before stacking them. "We can still do a bit more before the light goes."

The man put an arm around the woman's shoulder as they came out of the kitchen door and began stepping unevenly up the diagonal slope toward the stone wall and the line of trees. In his free hand he carried an axe. The boy followed them whistling. He had the two machetes with him. When they came to the lookout corner she stopped.

43

"Which tree did you mean?" the man asked.

"It's that popple—look—that tall one."

"Oh, yes—you're right. Yes, that would make a big difference. Funny we didn't notice it before."

The tree was one of the common field poplars people called popples, which grew almost as thick as alders in the neglected lands of a once-prosperous farming country. But where the alders were dull leaved and somehow shapeless, the little poplars were always graceful, and she loved their tremulous ways, the gray green of bark and leaves. In the upper pasture they advanced from the woods into the open in little lines as if hand in hand. They must not be allowed to take over, but a few should remain, to catch the light and the breezes. This one, however, grew not in the open grass but out of what was already a thicket of smaller popple, alder and bramble. The white blossom of the blackberry bushes glimmered in the fading light. The tree that was to be felled grew on the downslope but was tall enough to far overtop the line of the northeast horizon, and full enough to block off almost all of that swooping valley among the nearer hills beyond which lay the far-away mountains she longed to see.

The man and the boy after a moment's pause had gone on down the slope and were hidden now behind the bushes. The woman stood looking at the tree. The sun was just gone down, in back of her, but the eastern sky, which had clouded over while they were indoors, was not yet dark. Dove grays were flushed with wild-flower hues of mauve and pink, the white edges of high cumulus were veiled in transparent gold. The tree's gray green was still more green than gray. It stood at just such a distance from her that she could hear the voices of her husband and son, who were struggling now with the tangle of brush that surrounded it, but could not distinguish their words unless they shouted. As she looked, a rift in the clouds gave to the poplar's topmost branches a last gleam of sunlight which began almost immediately to fade. A thrill

44

of wind ran through the tree, and its leaves even in the dulled light flickered like sequins. No other tree picked up the wind until after the poplar had rippled with it, but as the poplar grew almost still again all the lower trees began to stir. The rustling passed from tree to tree until if she closed her eyes she could think herself on a pebble beach. It slowly hushed, a wave powerfully sucking small pebbles and shells with it in its retreat, and no wave succeeded it.

Now the man and the boy had evidently come right up to the trunk of the tree. By the sound of their voices she knew they were arguing about what angle to begin chopping from. A wood thrush was singing somewhere beyond them. The woman began to feel cold, and pulled down the rolled sleeves of her sweater, nervously. She was ill at ease. There was every reason for the tree to come down; she knew those mountains were more truly mountains than the nearer ones that could already be seen; they were more truly mountains not only because of their height and their defined forms but because of their distance. She knew that on days when a sense of triviality or of nagging anxiety beset her, the sight of them, so far removed from her, would give her courage. But the tree stood out from among the blur of many trees, differentiated, poised in air, a presence, and her word had condemned it. She had spoken so quickly; it had been as if she had heard herself speaking words she had not first spoken in herself. And at once these actions began. Could she not have retracted, not shown the tree—or put off showing it for tonight at least? Or even now she could go down the slope and beg off—he would disagree but he would respect her feeling; and the boy would laugh at her or be indignant at her caprice, but within himself he would understand!

The disputing voices were silent but something was delaying the use of the axe. Swishing and hacking sounds, the rustle of pushed-aside leaves, told her they were still cutting away the bushes near the trunk. "So the axe can swing free," she thought. She stood as if unable to move, crossing her arms tightly as the evening grew colder. Her husband was full of a new liveliness these days. He moved from his desk to the fields and back again with a new lightness, as if such transitions were easy or as if there were no question of transition, as if the use of the mind and the use of the body were all one rhythm. She knew that was good, that was the way life should be lived. Could she—with her persistent sense of the precariousness of happiness, the knife-edge balance of his confidence, of all sureness—could she run to him now with a plea to stop what she had begun? To stop, when it was as much in his concern for her needs as for any need of his own to see those particular mountains, that he was felling this tree?

And while she stood came the first blow of the axe. Thwock. The leaves of a poplar are never completely still; but as yet there was no increase in their rippling. Thwock. The tree seemed to her to grow taller, to stretch itself, to smile in the sequin freedom of its flickering leaves. Thwock. With the third blow the whole tree moved—the trunk with a convulsive jerk and the leaves and branches shuddering deeply.

There was a pause. A murmur of voices, the tree seeming to hold its breath. The woman brushed away insects that were biting her bare legs and buzzing around her ears. Another phrase came from the thrush, from further away. The colors were gone from the sky now; the light that remained was toneless. All the varied greens of the woods had become a single dull green. Should she go down close to the tree and see the axe breaking into it? She had never been close to it, never touched its trunk. Should she go back to the house, heat the water and wash the dishes? The tree was as good as felled now, it was too late to stop it. How fearful when possibility becomes irremediable fact! But she remained where she stood, sullenly enduring the biting of the flies and mosquitoes that had gathered around her, not even trying again to wave them away with a piece of bracken.

The blows of the axe resumed. At each blow the tree shook a little, but after that first great jerk and shudder it

46

was as if it only patiently awaited its fall. But how long it took! How could it take so long to hack through quite a slender stem? She heard her husband give a short roar through clenched teeth. Then it seemed the boy was taking a turn at the axe. The blows came hastily one after another, but not so loud. And now the man had the axe again—slowly, heavily, thwock. Thwock.

"Now!" came the boy's voice high and loud, a yell. Very slowly at first the tree began to lean away backwards, then with gathering momentum it was falling, had fallen. The crash was no louder than the sound a man or a large animal might make, shouldering roughly through the thicket. The man let out a low shout of triumph.

The woman began to run clumsily downhill toward them but caught her foot in something, stumbled, and stopped, her heart beating fast and a feeling of loneliness and confusion overwhelming her.

"Did you see it fall?" the boy cried, coming up to her, breathlessly.

"It was a lot tougher than I expected," her husband said, drawing near, smiling warmly and pushing the sweat off his forehead. He turned to see what had been revealed.

"Wow! That was worth doing. Just look at that!"

They gazed through and beyond the space the poplar had occupied. There to the northeast, in the scooped-out hollow of the pass, was an area of unclouded sky still pale with the last of daylight, and against it the far mountains were ranged, a wistful blue, remote and austere.

47

A photo of someone else's childhood,
a garden in another country—world
he had no part in and has no power to imagine:

yet the old man who has failed his memory
keens over the picture—'Them happy days—
gone—gone for ever!'—glad for a moment to suppose

a focus for unspent grieving, his floating
sense of loss.
He wanders

asking the day of the week, the time,
over and over the wrong questions.
Missing his way in the streets

he acts out
the bent of his life,
the lost way

never looked for, life
unlived, of which he is dying
very slowly.

'A man,'
says his son, 'who never
made a right move in all his life.' A man

who thought **the dollar was sweet** and
couldn't make a buck, riding the subway
year after year to untasted sweetness,

loving his sons obscurely, incurious
who they were, these men, his sons—
a shadow of love, for love longs

to know the beloved, and a light goes with it
into the dark mineshafts of feeling . . . A man
who now, without knowing,

in endless concern for the smallest certainties,
looking again and again at a paid bill,
inquiring again and again, 'When was I here last?'

asks what it's too late to ask:
'Where is my life? Where is my life?
What have I done with my life?'

Who Is at My Window

Who is at my window, who, who?
It's the blind cuckoo, mulling
the old song over.

The old song is about fear, about
tomorrow and next year.

Timor mortis conturbat me, he sings
What's the use?   He brings me

the image of **when,** a boat
hull down, smudged on the darkening ocean.

I want to move deeper into today;
he keeps me from that work.
Today and eternity are nothing to him.
His wings spread at the window make it dark.

Go from my window, go, go!

As if that hand
squeezing crow's blood
      against a white sky
      beside an idiot's laughing face
were real.

Having set out
in shoes that hurt
by the bog road
      and missed the way.

A cold day
dragging to a
      cold end.

The blood congealing
black
      between the pleased fingers.

In the Japanese
tongue of the
mind's eye one
two syllable word
tells of
the fringe of rain
clinging to the eaves
and of the grey-green
fronds of
wild parsley.

The world is
not with us enough.
O taste and see

the subway Bible poster said,
meaning **The Lord,** meaning
if anything all that lives
to the imagination's tongue,

grief, mercy, language,
tangerine, weather, to
breathe them, bite,
savor, chew, swallow, transform

into our flesh our
deaths, crossing the street, plum, quince,
living in the orchard and being

hungry, and plucking
the fruit.

No skilled hands
   caress a stranger's flesh with lucid oil before
a word is spoken
           no feasting
before a tale is told, before
the stranger tells his name.

The ships come and go
along the river and
in and out of the Narrows
and few among us know it

we are so many

   and many within themselves
travel to far islands but no one
asks for their story

nor is there an exchange of gifts, stranger
   to stranger
nor libation
nor sacrifice to the gods

and no house has its herm.

The river in its abundance
many-voiced
all about us as we stood
on a warm rock to wash

slowly
smoothing in long
                    sliding strokes
our soapy hands along each other's
slippery cool bodies

quiet and slow in the midst of
the quick of the
sounding river

our hands were
flames
stealing upon quickened flesh until

no part of us but was
sleek and
on fire

They enter the bare wood, drawn
by a clear-obscure summons they fear
and have no choice but to heed.

A rustling underfoot, a
long trail to go, the thornbushes grow
across the dwindling paths.

Until the small clearing, where they
anticipate violence, knowing some rite
to be performed, and compelled to it.

The man moves forward, the boy
sees what he means to do: from an oaktree
a chain runs at an angle into earth

and they pit themselves to uproot it,
dogged and frightened, to pull the iron
out of the earth's heart.

But from the further depths of the wood
as they strain and weigh on the great chain
appears the spirit,

the wood-demon who summoned them.
And he is not bestial, not fierce
but an old woodsman,

gnarled, shabby, smelling of smoke and sweat,
of a bear's height and shambling like a bear.
Yet his presence is a spirit's presence

56

and awe takes their breath.
Gentle and rough, laughing a little,
he makes his will known:

not for an act of force he called them,
for no rite of obscure violence
but that they might look about them

and see intricate branch and bark,
stars of moss and the old scars
left by dead men's saws,

and not ask what that chain was.
To leave the open fields
and enter the forest,

that was the rite.
Knowing there was mystery, they could go.
Go back now! And he receded

among the multitude of forms,
the twists and shadows they saw now, listening
to the hum of the world's wood.

Hand of man
hewed from
the mottled rock

almost touching
as Adam the hand of God

smallest inviolate
stone violet

When my body leaves me
I'm lonesome for it.
I've got

eyes, ears,
nose and mouth
and that's all.

Eyes
keep on seeing the
feather blue of the

cold sky,
mouth takes in
hot soup,
nose

smells the frost,

ears hear everything, all
the noises and absences,
but body

goes away to I don't know where
and it's lonesome to drift
above the space it
fills when it's here.

Bricks of the wall,
so much older than the house—
taken I think from a farm pulled down
     when the street was built—
narrow bricks of another century.

Modestly, though laid with panels and parapets,
a wall behind the flowers—
roses and hollyhocks, the silver
pods of lupine, sweet-tasting
phlox, gray
lavender—
     unnoticed—
         but I discovered
the colors in the wall that woke
when spray from the hose
played on its pocks and warts—

a hazy red, a
grain gold, a mauve
of small shadows, sprung
from the quiet dry brown—

         archetype
of the world always a step
beyond the world, that can't
be looked for, only
as the eye wanders,
found.

From the shrivelling gray
silk of its cocoon
a creature slowly
    is pushing out
to stand clear—
        not a butterfly,
           petal that floats at will across
           the summer breeze

        not a furred
        moth of the night
           crusted with indecipherable
           gold—

some primal-shaped, plain-winged, day-flying thing.

Take me or leave me, cries
Melody Grundy. I
like my face.
I am gaily alone.

On my cast-iron horse I was swiftly
everywhere, and no one
saw it for what it was.
That was romance. I leaned

on the mighty tree-stump to watch
an other life at play.
That was joy, I wept, I
leapt into my ship

to sail over grass. Melody
Plenty-of-Friends-Elsewhere
doesn't care,
will sing for all to hear.

Mountain, mountain, mountain,
marking time. Each
nameless, wall beyond wall, wavering
redefinition of
horizon.

And through the months. The arrivals
at dusk in towns one must leave at daybreak

—were they
taken to heart, to be seen
always again,
or let go, those faces,

a door half-open, moss
by matchlight on an inscribed stone?

And by day
through the hours that
rustle about one dryly,
tall grass of the savannah

up to the eyes.
No alternative to the
one-man path.

A wind is blowing. The book being written
shifts, halts, pages
yellow and white drawing apart
and inching together in
new tries. A single white half sheet
skims out under the door.

And cramped in their not yet
halfwritten lives, a man and a woman
grimace in pain. Their cat
yawning its animal secret,
stirs in the monstrous limbo of erasure.
They live (when they live) in fear

of blinding, of burning, of choking under a
mushroom cloud in the year of the roach.
And they want (like us) the eternity
of today, they want this fear to be
struck out at once by a thick black
magic marker, everywhere, every page,

the whole sheets of it crushed, crackling,
and tossed in the fire
and when they were fine ashes
the stove would cool and be cleaned
and a jar of flowers would be put to stand
on top of the stove in the spring light.

Meanwhile from page to page they
buy things, acquiring the look of a
full life; they argue, make silence bitter,
plan journeys, move house, implant
despair in each other
and then in the nick of time

they save one another with tears,
remorse, tenderness—
hooked on those wonder-drugs.
Yet they do have—
don't they—like us—
their days of grace, they

halt, stretch, a vision
breaks in on the cramped grimace,
inscape of transformation.
Something sundered begins to knit.
By scene, by sentence, something is rendered
back into life, back to the gods.

A form upon the quilted
overcast, gleam, Sacré
Coeur, saltlick
to the mind's
desire—

how shall the pulse
beat out
that measure,
under devious
moon
wander swerving

to wonder—

hands turn
what stone to uncover
feather of broken
oracle—

I slide my face along to the mirror
sideways, to see
that side-smile,
a pale look, tired
and sly. Hey,

who is glancing there?
Shadow-me, not with
malice but mercurially
shot with foreknowledge of
dread and sweat.

Don't lock me in wedlock, I want
marriage, an
encounter—

I told you about the
green light of
May

       (a veil of quiet befallen
       the downtown park,
       late

       Saturday after
       noon, long
       shadows and cool

       air, scent of
       new grass,
       fresh leaves,

       blossom on the threshold of
       abundance—

       and the birds I met there,
       birds of passage breaking their journey,
       three birds each of a different species:

       the azalea-breasted with round poll, dark,
       the brindled, merry, mousegliding one,
       and the smallest, golden as gorse and wearing
       a black Venetian mask

       and with them the three douce hen-birds
       feathered in tender, lively brown—

            I stood
            a half-hour under the enchantment,
            no-one passed near,
            the birds saw me and

            let me be
            near them.)

        It's not
        irrelevant:
        I would be
        met

        and meet you
        so,
        in a green

        airy space, not
        locked in.

Hypocrite women, how seldom we speak
of our own doubts, while dubiously
we mother man in his doubt!

And if at Mill Valley perched in the trees
the sweet rain drifting through western air
a white sweating bull of a poet told us

our cunts are ugly—why didn't we
admit we have thought so too? (And
what shame? They are not for the eye!)

No, they are dark and wrinkled and hairy,
caves of the Moon . . .   And when a
dark humming fills us, a

coldness towards life,
we are too much women to
own to such unwomanliness.

Whorishly with the psychopomp
we play and plead—and say
nothing of this later.   And our dreams,

with what frivolity we have pared them
like toenails, clipped them like ends of
split hair.

There's in my mind a woman
of innocence, unadorned but

fair-featured, and smelling of
apples or grass. She wears

a utopian smock or shift, her hair
is light brown and smooth, and she

is kind and very clean without
ostentation—
                    but she has
no imagination.
                    And there's a
turbulent moon-ridden girl

or old woman, or both,
dressed in opals and rags, feathers

and torn taffeta,
who knows strange songs—

but she is not kind.

Our bodies, still young under
the engraved anxiety of our
faces, and innocently

more expressive than faces:
nipples, navel, and pubic hair
make anyway a

sort of face: or taking
the rounded shadows at
breast, buttock, balls,

the plump of my belly, the
hollow of your
groin, as a constellation,

how it leans from earth to
dawn in a gesture of
play and

wise compassion—
nothing like this
comes to pass
in eyes or wistful
mouths.
      I have

a line or groove I love
runs down
my body from breastbone
to waist. It speaks of
eagerness, of
distance.

        Your long back,
the sand color and
how the bones show, say

what sky after sunset
almost white
over a deep woods to which

rooks are homing, says.

Long after you have swung back
away from me
I think you are still with me:

you come in close to the shore
on the tide
and nudge me awake the way

a boat adrift nudges the pier:
am I a pier
half-in half-out of the water?

and in the pleasure of that communion
I lose track,
the moon I watch goes down, the

tide swings you away before
I know I'm
alone again long since,

mud sucking at gray and black
timbers of me,
a light growth of green dreams drying.

At Delphi I prayed
to Apollo
that he maintain in me
the flame of the poem

and I drank of the brackish
spring there, dazed by the
gong beat of the sun,
mistaking it,

as I shrank from the eagle's
black shadow crossing
that sky of cruel blue,
for the Pierian Spring—

and soon after
vomited my moussaka
and then my guts writhed
for some hours with diarrhea

until at dusk
among the stones of the goatpaths
breathing dust
I questioned my faith, or

within it wondered
if the god mocked me.
But since then, though it flickers or
shrinks to a

blue bead on the wick,
there's that in me that
burns and chills, blackening
my heart with its soot,

flaring in laughter, stinging
my feet into a dance, so that
I think sometimes not Apollo heard me
but a different god.

October

Certain branches cut
certain leaves fallen
the grapes
        cooked and put up
for winter

mountains without one
shrug of cloud
no feint of blurred
wind-willow leaf-light

their chins up
in blue of the eastern sky
their red cloaks
wrapped tight to the bone

Let me walk through the fields of paper
touching with my wand
dry stems and stunted
butterflies—

let Sluggard Acre send up
sunflowers among its weeds,
ten foot high—let its thistles
display their Scottish magnificence,
mauve tam-o'-shanters and barbed plaids—

yes, set fire to frostbitten crops,
drag out forgotten fruit
to dance the flame-tango,
the smoke-gavotte,
to live after all—

let the note **elephant** become a song,
the white beast wiser than man
raise a dust in the north woods,
loping on corduroy roads to the arena.

A March

'. . . in those wine- and urine-stained
hallways, something in me wondered, *What will happen to all that
black beauty?*'
                                James Baldwin

Out of those hallways
crossing the street to blue
astonished eyes

as though by first light
made visible, dark
presences slowly
focus

revelation of
tulip blacks, delicate
browns, proportion
of heavy lip to bevelled
temple bone

       The mind
of a fair man at the intersection
jars
at the entering of this
beauty, filing

endlessly through his blue
blinking eyes into
the world within him

I could replace
God for awhile, that old ring of candles,
that owl's wing brushing the dew
off my grass hair.
If bended knee calls up
a god, if the imagination of idol
calls up a god, if melting
of heart or what was written as
bowels but has to do
                 not with shit but with salutation of
                 somber beauty in what is mortal,
calls up a god by recognition and power of
longing, then in my forest
God is replaced awhile,
awhile I can turn from that slow embrace
to worship *mortal,* the summoned
god who has speech, who has wit
to wreathe all words, who laughs
wrapped in sad pelt and without hope of heaven,
who makes a music turns the heads
of all beasts
as mine turns, dream-hill grass
standing on end at echo even.

There are weeds that flower forth in fall
in a gray cloud of seed that seems
from a not so great distance
plumblossom, pearblossom,
or first snow,

as if in a fog of feather-light
goosedown-silvery seed-thoughts
a rusty mind in its autumn
reviewed, renewed
its winged power.

My great brother
　　Lord of the Song
wears the ruff of
　　forest bear.

Husband, thy fleece of silk is black,
　　　　a black adornment;
lies so close to the turns of the flesh,
burns my palm-stroke.

My great brother
　　Lord of the Song
wears the ruff of
　　forest bear.

Strong legs of our son are dusted
　　　　dark with hair.
Told of long roads,
we know his stride.

My great brother
　　Lord of the Song
wears the ruff of
　　forest bear.

Hair of man, man-hair, hair of
breast and groin, marking contour as
　　silverpoint marks in cross-
　　hatching, as river-
　　grass on the woven current
　　indicates ripple,
praise.

*(These words were given me in a
dream. In the dream I was a Finnish
child of 8 or 9 who had been given
by her teacher the task of writing
out these 3 ancient runes of her
people. This is how they went:)*

(1) Know the pinetrees. Know the orange dryness of sickness
and death in needle and cone. Know them too in green health,
those among whom your life is laid.

(2) Know the ship you sail on. Know its timbers. Deep the
fjord waters where you sail, steep the cliffs, deep into the unknown coast goes the winding fjord. But what would you
have? Would you be tied up to a sandwhite quay in perpetual
sunshine, yards and masts sprouting little violet mandolins?

(3) In city, in suburb, in forest, no way to stretch out the
arms— so if you would grow, go straight up or deep down.